In Silence 8 Tears

A Selection of Poems

In Silence & Tears
A Selection of Poems

Jeffrey Gomez

Nom de Plume Publishing
2017

First Printing: 2017

ISBN 978-0-692-35544-2

Library of Congress Control Number: 2017913734

Nom de Plume Publishing
Pasadena, California 91107

Dedication

This book is dedicated to the girl who broke my heart.
Thank you.

Contents

Preface

The collection of poems presented in this book represent a span of four years in my life. During that time I experienced every emotion one could hope to happen. From the existential feeling of love to the darkest hours of heartbreak and depression, every emotion is laid out before you. I do not shy away from pain or hurt. I use these powerful feelings to explore my own self. To be comfortable with ones short-comings and talents, is to experience life to its fullest. I have, since the age of fourteen, been a writer. I simply could not find any other way to clear the thoughts that ran so rampant in my head than through poetry. The best way I can describe "getting the feeling to write", is as if my head is full of thoughts, like a barrel about to overflow with water. So I rush to my handy pen and paper and let the words flow out, thus relieving my soul.

I chose this collection of poetry as my first foray into publishing simply for the fact that out of the hundreds of poems that I have written, this time period seems, up to this point, to be my most prolific time period of writing. I do not write every single day. In fact, there are times when I can go months or a year without writing a single word. I can only account for this spacing as not being inspired or being so drawn into other affairs that my brain is engaged elsewhere.

Sadly, poetry is now merely a footnote within the education system. However, I still move forward with this style of writing. It simply should not be lost to history. And it incenses me to think that poetry is so forgotten and belittled in this day and age. Though I do have to admit that most modern poetry is pure self-loathing drivel. Sometimes I even get sick of myself! The greats of the Romantic period and up until the early 20th century should definitely be further revered for their long and lasting legacies of syntax.

Upon turning the page and beginning your journey into my life and soul, you will see that some words, punctuation and spelling is missing or incorrect. As an iconoclastic writer who doesn't want to follow the traditional mores of poetry, I have written as I see fit and the mood that reflects that time. I feel that having these boundaries, set a poem to be read only one way, when in fact, whatever you the reader are feeling, can impart your spirit into the poem and take away what you need in that moment. Poetry is a living and breathing entity. It should not have to be confined to such human constraints.

One final thought I want to share with readers is that though this collection seems rather bleak on its face, my life is a cacophony of colors and wonder. Poetry seems to spring mostly from frustration and pain for me, but there are bright spots as well. I used to think that poetry was only made from the pain of writers, until I forced myself to read a myriad of poets from around the world. Each of us is different and the emotions that call us to action are different as well. My life is an ever evolving movie of the greatest proportions. So worry for me not. I am just like you, with facets and details on this wonderful journey we call life!

My meditations are but momentary

The flurry in my head

Keeps me up 'til daylight

Writing the words He said

I approach the mornings with a vigor

Loving this life and the one

That is yet to come ahead

So I take solace that the restbit

I've missed in this bed

Will come soon enough

Once of course I'm dead!

2:29am

9/1/09

Death is my ally

For he lets me see beauty

In the daily struggles

And personal slights

I find I am alive

To feel the sting of rebuke

The bittersweet taste of a high romance

And the blackness of a sorrowful loss

A multitude of emotions

The agonized truth revealed

To my own forgetful head

This is when I know

That I am not already dead

2:15am

9/10/09

The hurricane is comin'

Are you ready?

Did you grab the tangible goods

That represent your life?

The objects of your being

That tell the narrative

To you- your only audience?

Don't forget the incongruous

Those which have no form

The memories and the thoughts

Bittersweet failures and the ripened grain

Of a wondrous success

Keep these in the forefront

'Lest the tide rise so high

And wash away even you

And in that final aching breath

The extinguishment of life

You have no reflection, meditation

Or gratitude

For the flicker of your flame

Yes! The hurricane is comin'

Are you ready?

1:09pm

11/29/09

Oh! How I chase that elusive gift

Buried within my doubtful mind

Many have seen his eager eye

The flint rock to the fire

Of success and wealth abound

Yet I have seen him not

And am looking at the ground

Myself I chastise when I see

That- the other side of me

Pompous and proud announced

Of all the things I have

And all I will be

'Til reality- the subtle thief of pride

Nicks the platform of my place

So let me rest interassuréd

That what I may hold

Inside the crevasses of my mind

Need my middle Thomas

Lest a great me I find

1:27am

12/12/09

If I had within my heart

Your conviction of our art

T'would be different

If I urged that fancy thought

And spilled the contents of my soul

To you- my missing part

Would you hold?

Or dash me against the rocks

Lifeless on the shore

Of an unrequited love?!

'Tis misery in both beleaguered bends

So I hasten not

To make us more than friends

But if I knew

You seek the same design

I'd gladly pay the ransom of a king

To spend with you

The waking of each day

Yet here I sit

Too petrified to protest

The crimes against my heart

And there we sit

Miles and miles apart

My only solace

This poem- my only art

How shall I proceed?

2:10am

12/12/09

Bereft of breath

And the comfort of your voice

My! How times been cruel

To me- a tattered fool

The errors of my words

And the thoughtless self promotion

Of this- my bitter mirror

So here I lie

My humility all aglow

Bearing witness to my folly

To that- your empty line

11:36pm

12/16/09

In this life

The hours march their endless pace

Ceasing for nothing- til nothingness succeeds

I therefore do not ask

For the account of your past

It is in the here and now

And the future yet to come

That I ask for this

A solemn gift

One of no compare

To hold your hand

-And cusp your heart

To reap the greatest gift

And slay that awful beast

Of solitude and misery

So take my trembling hand

Be my breath renewed

Together we shall reap

The riches of a life complete

12:06am

3/23/10

My heart hangs its heavy soul

Upon my broken chest

Thinking it tried it all

And did its very best

But fickle you- the subtle thief of life

Quelched the hopes and the dreams

You who I thought I'd call wife

So here I lay

Unrequited in my love

Despiséd more instead

I fear to answer further

To further slide my chances

Of ever receiving those gifts I adore

That of your loving glances

Here is a small approbation

My loves dimming light

Waiting for that day

You choose to reunite

12:20am

3/23/10

I lost my friend today

The precious jewel of my heart

The sinew of my soul

Has been stripped from its start

I am- an empty vassal

Too bottomless to fill

My baby is gone today

And I have nothing left to feel

Too numbed by the pain

Too angered by that Death

The one I want to kill

10:54pm

3/29/10

My life has ceased today

The path has gone away

I lost the footing and the hold

On the existence of my plane

I was stifled by that Death

And the abruptness of his work

Yet there are miracles

Yes! Miracles indeed

By the God in the heaven above

That knows when we are in need

For he saved my through and through

By bringing me divination

The calm of a loving heart

11:02pm

3/29/10

I know clear as the clearest day

That she is the One

The one who touched my heart

As I opened my boundless realm

And the delicate nature that surrounds my feeble heart

And unfurled the cavalcade

Of the darkest distress

And the brightest joy

The vicissitudes of my being

She was there

Like the calm of a gentle wind

That whispers in your ear

"All is good," she said

And assuaged away my fear

11:09pm

3/29/10

Here is a tiny testament

To you- my greatest treasure

That my life, thus far

Is hapless

When put against your measure

The brief hours and weeks

Since you stole my heart complete

Has left me tranquil

And assured

My love will not deplete

So seek not an understanding

That makes mortals of men

And find comfort in your heart

My word will never bend

For I chase the fleeting day

And ask her for more time

Knowing that anything less

Is truly the greatest crime

Believe in these things- my promises-

Written here

So when that darkness named doubt

Plies his awful trade

You will know- without question

My love will never fade

1:15am

4/8/10

I don't want you to-

Simply fade away

I don't want to be-

That facet of a thought

That may linger in a moment

Nay! I long for that-

Tangible feeling

Stopping you in your tracks

I want that indelible mark

To be us-

Such as we are

5/15/10

Understand yet!

The trifles and the petty

Of what they call love

Is not for our collective

Arguments and cursed words

Silent nights and the blackest moods

Sit idly by

Hoping for their slight chances

To fell that perfect steeple

Erect in his true form

Showing to the world

A proclamation- a validation

That we ourselves have been true

To our faces in the mirror

And the reflections in our eyes

Not time

Nor space

Can separate our will

And so we shall

Carry forward

The finding of a fruitful heart

And smile upon the day

-And years

Aeons still unspent

'Til when it all comes to pass

We barely made our start

1:57am

6/26/10

I am the watchman

Of fervent thought

Who is tasked with catching

That elusive phrase

Who, like a thoroughbred all astride

Rushes for the line

Of fleeting moment

And sagacious syntax

That He himself

Has divined

A simple medium

Conduit reposed

Of an average man

So with awestruck eyes

And an open heart

I stand and tend my post

4:02am

6/20/10

I have a weight upon my shoulders

A worry in my mind

I stare- at the blank page

And the horizon for to see

The questions

The lingering questions

'Bout what I'm supposed to be

I have no answers

So I look down

At my feet

Whose simple motion is constant

On this- the only road I know

1:37am

7/9/10

Oh Lord!

I beseech you

To guide me from this

A mess- my life

I have stumbled

And fallen

I am a person- I know not

How I yearn to be

Someone other than me

Free and unburdened

Alack! I am not

So I sit here

Praying to you

Please continue

Revealing the me

I will be

1:48am

7/9/10

What is love?

With the reasoning of a simple mind

Love is that everlasting day

It is the warmth of the summer's breeze

The thought and dreams of an endless fancy

But nay-

That is not truthful love

For it can be found

Though incongruous to us

In the moment

And the wasted breath

It needs not spring from an eternal pond

Or chase the songbird of tomorrow

12:40am

7/29/10

We like to push past

The lonesome hours

And the dawn of tomorrow

With clinking glasses

And boisterous laughs

We forget, if for a night

The reality of our lives

And it's sad to see

The irony-

That makes us delirious kids

Awash in a game of pretend

We are but humans

With a fallacy

Of what life could be

If we lacked that bit of us

The soul that makes us free

12:54am

8/8/10

If I have led you down a path

Most unrighteous-

Or have squandered our light

Into the dimmest of brightness

If I have written words

Of actions- sedentary

And have lived our life

In that beguiling familiarity

If all these things

Which vex you now

-Hold- I shall take my bow

So with that last and lumbering breath

I will share the one resolve

For when the trumpet sounds

And people shuffle to their lives

When you, solitary on that hill

Overlook that majesty

Know that gentle wind

Which caresses your neck

And fades with one triumphant flutter

My love lives within

Words I wish to mutter

3:21am

8/29/10

In this large engrossing world wide

Where thoughts hang over the expanse of opportunity

Where secret dreams are laid bare

And all the fear we hold inside

Melts into nothingness

-I sit and stare

For my life and that of thee

And all the things we could be

If- for each of those moments

Where hesitation becomes king

And trepidation- his right hand

We triumphed

What a beauteous vision

I can see

If and when

We slay that bitter self

Of what we only wish to be

1:32am

11/28/10

I burn for you

Blood surges through my veins

As I ponder a position

My body stands erect

With the rhythmic and fast pace of my heartbeat

-The only movement you see

I want you closer

I want to taste your delights

The warm and supple skin

Engrossing my face

Free! Your mind and body

Relinquish control for the moment

And shutter in the ecstasy

Explode in the night

So let us partake

You and I

Of the animalistic urges

Let us feast on the pleasures of our naked bodies

And slumber the deepest sleep

From an exhausted and sticky fight

10:46pm

1/10/11

There is a stillness in a kiss

For that moment- when lips are locked

And all the world falls silent

That's a bit of heaven

And so we share

A gift of refuge

A meeting of the divine

Plunging in – eyes closed

For yet another time

9:36 pm

1/14/11

There is still a longing

A long encompassing embrace

That floats upon love

And the nothingness of bliss

Where time and circumstance

Fall to the wayside

It is what I seek

The warmth from a depth

A quieting to my mind

To live – in that brief moment

A reality of dreams

Fortified in the simplicity

Of a pure and genuine love

11:47 pm

2/8/11

I want you to be a woman

To exude your sexuality

Feel that comfort of your skin

And the attributes of your sex

Take refuge in my presence

-Use it to solidify that person

The one who turns the heads

And brightens her own mirror

Let all the present

All the humdrum days

And worrisome tasks

-Lose focus

To be but a backdrop

For us

For you

And that titillating goddess within

4-14-11

1:44am

I'm being cheated, again

By you- the one who won't commit

I sit here alone

As the hours fly by

As my life and all the world around me

Continues its course

Yet here I am

With memories and thoughts

Of you, you treasonous ghost

Too bitter is your taste

As my still broken heart

Hurts some more

I wish I could give you up

As you did me

And stop this anguish

To finally be free

9-26-11

12:26am

I promise you this-

With my words and ego

My familiar emotions

The "you" I know

And my trust in God

This isn't it.

So drink up while the night is young

Revel in the new and fertile fields

Seek the attentions that make you smile

For they are but illusions

Wishful thinking at its best

You know- As I do

Convictions of the heart

Are matters we cannot change

So when you've had your fill

And tire of the facades

When you've been cheated and belittled

Compromised by the capricious

Turn your ear towards me

And listen for the sound

It is our march-

The beat you drowned with selfishness

Yes- it still plays

By one who knows the truth

Now further still today

Can you catch up?

Or did it leave you while you played?

10-6-11

12:03am

And so she goes

To walk the new man out

And closes the door behind him

When she realizes truth.

That sex without emotion

Is lust.

It is a carnal diversion

Too shallow to be worthy.

Yet sex with love, sparks and intimacy

Is nobler still.

And so she goes

To the shower to cleanse

Her body and her mind

The hot steam rises

Like the thoughts she's having

A flurry in her head.

It is when she towels off

And wipes the foggy mirror

That she stares at the truth

In her face

that it is He

The one she threw away

The one she betrayed and broke

And swore to hate

He is the one that got away.

Alack! She is mired now

In the bog of her design

To experience the anguish

Of the many, the pompous

The timewasters and the liars

It is He I say

Her true soulmate

The one that got away

12-6-11

4:05am

Oh, glorious drink!

You bewitching devil in a cup

How I pine for your attention

How I seek your rationale

To make it all better

To make it all right

You are a scourge

Upon my body, relationships and my reputation

Yet I seek you still

Take me away, fly me from this reality

I want the laughter and the times

Make me lose the now

"One more", I say

'Til I, arrested in my stupor

Understand I can never run away

7-6-12

1:22am

I am so forlorn

In these quiet hours

Where others clamour to and fro

To drink, to meet friends, to fuck

"Not me", says I

The scared and despondent self I know

From the foolish, dangerous and expensive

Lessons learned

So here I sit- alone

Aloof from a life I knew

Pushed further from society

It is so dreary here

And I wish I could control me

But experience says no

So you, dear paper and pen

Shall keep my confidence.

9-1-12

1:29am

A little piece of me broke *that* day

Time has since pushed *tha*t day-

Further from my memory

The pain has not left

It sits- as a guard

To assess my actions

My everyday

I am torn

By myself and the system

I lost my innocence *that* day

A bit of myself shattered

I wish I could go back

To be whole

To be me once more

9-3-12

1:59am

God did not forsake Job

Nor did He me

Nay, I stumbled

And careened down my path

To where I am now

'Tis easier to blame Him

For He does not show

'Tis easier still to rebuke HIm

For He does not speak

How foolish

Yet for the fool in me

He will carry me through today

As He has done

And will always do

9-3-12

2:10am

Is there really a defect to me

That I should be alone still?

Is there no talent

Which is enticing enough to save me?

What do I lack that makes

Women, relations, people nothing more

Than flickers of my flame?

I need a foundation

Dearly- let me land on solid footing

Priceless is that want

For a woman

For a hand

An open heart

9-3-12

2:17am

Luke, I am not

For I cannot be so middle ground

I've tried- In all I do

To be but a body or number

'Til in protest- louder still

'Tis not my nature, to sit silent

Nay, my life is a stirring fire

Too busy to be quelched

Too proud to be led

So seek not a companion in me

Nor compatriot for cause

'Lest your name is

-Luke

9-6-12

2:16am

Have no pity for me

I am just a fool

One who makes nothing

From the talents he's been given

How do I explain?

Is there a way to reason

Why my life is thus?

Motivation- she is my elusive spark

A sprite, hard to catch

I could be so much more

One rich in friends, fortune and fame

But she eludes me still

And I-

I am those too oft heard words

"One rich in promise"

But nothing more

9-6-12

2:30am

My life is so bleak most days

When the sun winds down

And friends go their merry way

I am left- alone once more -

To sit in silence

With me, my only confidant

How dreary it is

To be without Her- the One -

Where does she reside?

How do I move closer

With no compass foretosee?

Hold fast my lonely heart

Be burdened no more

For another night is almost over

9-16-12

10:47pm

Nobody knows my melancholy

Nor do I

It comes and goes and comes again

From the depths of a great despair

For want of love, life and money

All that I've failed at

And all I want to be

Nobody knows this side of me

So here I lay

Suffering in silence

Lamenting and wanting-

Wondering and hoping

For what tomorrow will bring

9-16-12

11:07pm

I want you to love me

And me you

To be each others thought provoked

Squeezing, with all strength contained

Every ounce of this sweet life.

I want to wear your scent

And you mine

As a badge of devotion

A fragrant reminder

That we are loved.

I want you to hold me

And me you

In the darkness of night

To share our fears and slights

As sages to each other

Wisdom be our might.

I want to romance your mind

And you mine

To speak volumes of issues, contradictions and life

To hear the tranquility of your voice

Honesty in every word

Nothing left unspoken.

I want you to find me

And me you

To transcend the barren lands

Of life and death

Eternity-

Our loves true Spring.

9-16-12

11:47pm

I am sifting through the wreckage

That is my current life

There be no gold here- amidst the shards

Nay, only dizzy dreams of an innocent child

That flew away

Only a speck on the horizon

What has come of me?

Where did it all go?

When did it all die?

These are the burning questions

That keep my nights long

Oh! The stress

-Showing face of a failed life

To her, to them, to myself

How do I grasp success

To turn this around

To bury this phase

Let me be blind no more

11-24-12 3:12am

My heart tells me

That she is anguished

So I, softly in the night

Say, "tell me more"

And so we lay

Staring into oblivion

Recounting, like a reel crackling in the dark,

The tumult of our trails

I, too meager to gift

And she, too hurt to feel

Share the same void

They say misery loves company

Nay. For we know too well

That fear and failure

In love-

Is all we need of Heaven

And all we know of Hell

12-18-12

12:40am

I possess you only in my past

And what is a future

Without you in my present?

Time goes by

And the hurt is forgotten

I daydream once more

Toward the bright and beaming promise.

So close it was

As the noon tide reaches shore

'Til I, foolish being complete

Lost her again and yes, once more

So silence shall be my companion

Solitude my bed

'Til that one day, in hope

You too, can forget

The vile things I said

12-18-12

1:15am

Oh, to be burdened no more

For 2012 is coming to a close

I feel, an old familiar friend

Coming back to me once more

Hope-

These 365 days have been some of my worst

Embarrassed, sad and despondent I have been

For too long

So as the clock strikes 12

And the world revels in the year

I shall sit here, quietly happy

And outwardly proud

That I have survived

Not with a fanfare or wild night

But a simple exhale

2012 shall be nevermore

My slate shall be cleansed

And a new life of hope and wisdom

One of promise and work

A daily occupation

To make 2013-

The best my life has ever had

Will begin

12-31-12 11:37pm

Oh, deceitful heart

You have led me once more

Down a path of unrequited love

How anguished am I now

Lonesome still to be

For the girl you said

Who was the one

Doesn't want that part of me

So here I sit

And her across the way

Making conscious effort

To hurry this awkward day

I wish this wasn't so

The dance we do today

For when intimacy binds us

We all should have to play

1-18-13

9:02am

I met a man in class tonight

Steven, was his name

And he was hurt

And lost-

And lonely-

And he was a drunk.

I watched him,

As he sat, staring at his life,

Questioning how he got there-

In a class of foolish boys,

Parading as men,

-Alcoholics Anonymous they call it.

It was then,

That I began to cry.

For I knew his story,

Too nearer than to tell,

'Bout the anguish in the mirror,

The all consuming darkness of night.

I wanted to speak his name

And give him one delight,

That he- in silence was worthy

To save this one fool's fight.

His eyes were a showcase to me

And his pain more palpable than petty,

Saying this was indeed me.

All the transgressions of my life,

A culmination of sin-

Sitting there too,

In front of him

And myself.

1-23-13

6:41pm

I wish I had something to live for

Cause I, myself, am not enough

Someone, something-

To call my very own

That loves and adores and sees beyond my faults

I cannot

So the motivation to keep on is nigh

And I go nowhere

-Still

2/5/13

12:52am

And there I had it!

All the words, emotions and sleepless nights

-Laid bare before her

I stopped my shaking hands and trembling voice

To spill my honest struggle- naked

-As she sees me

-As she has always known

Oh, glorious God in the heaven above

Who allowed me my humblest wish

-To see her one last time

How she shall live with me

In all thoughts and quiet hours

The keeper to my heart

-Most ardently

Let this therefore be for her

For my hour today was enough

And a reel in perpetua shall play

To remember her

-Us

To know that I

-She

-We

Are loved

2-25-13

12:12am

Oh, happy heart!

For you have seen her

And relished in the delight

Of a heavenly form

-An angelic being complete

Pray tell, how foolish did you look?

How clumsy was your syntax,

When standing before such a soul?

Did you wring out your heart

And share the multitude of your verse?

Did she hear and understand,

Your accounts before today?

Unfathomable it shall be

If you forgot as follows   .

-I love you

I love you

I love you

2-25-13

12:22am

---

fragment

It's finished!

The book of me and her.

We wrote the last chapter today

And so it is

That tonight is revisions of the words

Reading line for line

The words we did speak

Yes, we closed the chapter

And folded back the cover

So here I sit, and her there

Analyzing those precious few moments

2/25/13

Why is there a deficit to me

That leaves me as such

-Feeble

I am depressed and still

With neither motion or feeling

About the life that passes me by

So I implore myself

And cry to the heaven above

Why dost thou forsake me?!

I've heard no answer but,

"Be as you are".

So I shall push forward

Cautiously optimistic

That I am for something more

4/25/13

10:52pm

I'm lonely really

And embarrassed-

Cause I am nothing

And I have neither talent or degree

Occupation or house

To provide a value or benchmark to me

Nay, it is what you see

Simply me

So put not your time in this fellow

For he is to be pitied

Shunned further from your orbit

So says my sedentary body

So says my lying mouth

Forget these feelings and humility!

I need to rise

And awaken the genius within

To be me

All of me

The real and true Jeffrey

4/25/13

11:00pm

I can find no words

Nor know of a language so beauteous

To share with you

The burning of my heart

For you are the one

The angel of my days

Who heaven brought

To share with me- these days

Let us escape together

And break these solemn bonds

Of a sullied past

Carried by the winds of chance

Aloft in the reality of a dream

That we are one

Forged in the hellfire of a liar's scheme

Shaped by the battering waves of animosity

And polished by eternal truth

So take my hand dearest love

Summon the courage and conviction

Which comes from divine knowledge

That we are right

Jump with me

Jump, jump, jump

4/25/13

11:16pm

It is a scary proposition,

To share the me I am,

With someone new.

We've met but once.

And I, now in quiet reflection,

Doubt the things we shared.

Tis' bitter anguish,

The second guessing mind.

So here I sit,

The eve of our next encounter,

Petrified for my heart.

Was it real?

Will your actions follow your words,

Or shall the sting of hypocrisy

Numb me once again?

I know not these answers,

But am rooting for you now,

For me,

For us,

That we may strike the flame!

4-30-13

1:15am

That which we want

Is only beset by our own self doubt.

What the future holds,

In her promising, unripened grain,

Is beyond the purview of our imaginations.

So let us depart,

-You and I,

To savor the sweetness of each day,

To feel accomplished with each step.

Let us live this life together

And journey down those paths,

Over the undulating circumstances,

Beyond the horizon fortosee,

Into that eternity,

The constant of forever

-Loved

5-28-13

11:00pm

Why do I cry for you

When I'm in your oh so distant past?

Why do I think upon our times

When you make inroads with another?

Oh! Grievous mind

How you hurt me so

With the remembrances of her

Our perfect relationship

Now but a dream long since forgot

Yet here I lay

In the rut of a depresséd state

Longing for her.

My tears--

All that I have now

6-26-13

2:51am

I lay awake most nights

Reflecting upon our past

How odious to think

And how acute the pain

To know our race was run.

We lost-

And all the nighttide,

While you venture far and wide,

Meeting the gentlemen and snakes,

Awash in the caprice of strangers,

I lament.

But pray broken heart

Hold fast-

For we have something more

Heaven and Earth cannot refund

Our quiet times together.

Those, which behind curtain

And hidden in the dark

We shared

So let me keep these,

In the forefront of my delusion

That I may quell my tears

And you-

Yes, you who were but mine

Though nothing more today

Go seek thee something else

Cause I vow to do the same

Though honestly

I just lie.

7-12-13

2:44am

If I can hold

This week within my hands

I'd keep it forever

And replay the days

For here-

Within this time and circumstance

You're mine

Without reservation or distraction

Without the world

And its ways

We live a life unrivaled

Yet lesser now each day

So before you depart tomorrow

And onto your own way

Know that this time

Has been more than I can say

You are the individual

The one to keep in mind

For when all the folly surrounds me

You are the march of the divine

8-17-13

11:35pm

Oh unrequitedness

How terrible the sting

When here I lay

Just inches away

From her- the one

With nary a thing to say

She wants but none of me

But superficial fantasy

Or rather me of her

And all that we could be

But none of it

I shall get

For its only one way

So this night and circumstance

Will end as it began

With me forlorn- in the dark-

Only inches away

12:30am

8-18-13

I hate myself

For this

-The situation

Look at her

And all you see

Lying peacefully

While I

-Angry and awake

Chide my foolish self

For creating this whole day

I want to tell her more

And all my heart contain

But different her

Tis' not why she came

So let me hold my tongue

To keep the awkward silence

It's misery in each moment

But better than to say

12:38am 8-18-13

I am haunted by my past

The one I only see in pictures now

For the memories have faded from my mind

And yet, as I look upon the images I remember only pain

A sudden sense of longing and embarrassment are all I have left

Oh, those glorious times when life was grand

And each day was another adventure, in love

But they are all gone now

And I sit here, alone, with nothing more

Than these stinging bites of a life that is no more

Lord, how do I reclaim my life

How do I move from this most deservéd rut?

I am wallowing to no one

Crying a bootless lamentation to me

Do you even hear?

Let me drop these pictures

And turn myself away from that me

Who is so foreign now

In the stillness of this sad night let me cease this current path

With daybreak dear God, let me wake up

As someone else

And stop the foolishness that was

From repeating his awful yarn

10-2-13

1:14am

Yes, I saw you the other day

And I was swallowed-- whole--

By a wave of remembrances

Of a time long since past

Years now in fact.

And yet, in that one brief second

When eyes were locked

I ran the marathon

--The marathon of life's gamut

The joy and sadness, hope and fear

That grew from our terminal spring.

I relived the first glimpse of you

From across that ballroom floor

And relished in the happy times,

Those quiet moments in the night

Where I held you and breathed you in

So palpable a love this world had never seen

And yet, so precious more those instances

When fear was conquered and our feeblest selves supported

But acrimonious heart be still

For I also relived the darkest days

When these lips did lie

And this heart did cower into black

I tasted, solemnly once more

That bitter drink, I myself did concoct

The derision to division-- indeed --

So know that the distance maintained

And shall we meet again I will uphold

For my sins -- a line

To keep you free from that which consumed me

I tried, in vain did I try

To see just that light

We lit so long ago

But the world has forced us further still

From that familiar shore

Take care my love

I shall do the same

If and when fate brings us about

Think on this

This and nothing more

10/19/13

1:01am

Notes

www.ingramcontent.com/pod-product-compliance
Lightning Source LLC
Chambersburg PA
CBHW031001090426
42737CB00008B/623